THE POWER OF OF RESILIENCE

A JOURNEY OF HEALING AND SURVIVAL

CHARMAINE ANNA NCUBE

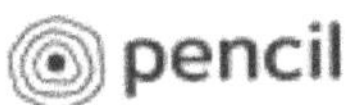

pencil

ISBN 978-93-5667-870-5
© CHARMAINE ANNA NCUBE 2023

Published in India 2023 by Pencil

A brand of
One Point Six Technologies Pvt. Ltd.
Unit no. 26, Ground Floor, Building A1,
Wadala Truck Terminal Road,
Near Post Office, Antop Hill, Mumbai - 400037
E connect@thepencilapp.com
W www.thepencilapp.com

DISCLAIMER: *The opinions expressed in this book are those of the authors and do not purport to reflect the views of the Publisher.*

Author biography

[Charmaine Anna Ncube], a brilliant wordsmith and a courageous soul, is the author behind the captivating and empowering novel [The Power of Resilience]. Born with an innate storytelling gift, [Charmaine Anna Ncube] weaves words into poignant tapestries that touch the hearts and minds of readers, leaving an indelible mark on their souls.Hailing from [Bulawayo Zimbabwean], [Charmaine Anna Ncube] drew inspiration from their own extraordinary life journey to craft a narrative that transcends the boundaries of fiction. With a deep-rooted passion for uplifting others, they fearlessly delved into the depths of their experiences, unearthing painful memories and transforming them into a beacon of hope and resilience.[Charmaine Anna Ncube]'s unwavering commitment to authenticity and emotional depth shines through every line of their writing. Their skilled use of dictionary words paints vivid landscapes of the human experience, evoking a myriad of emotions that resonate with readers on a profound level. The rich tapestry of their prose invites readers to step into the shoes of the protagonist, immersing themselves in a world of triumphs, trials, and transformation.Through the pages of [The Power of Resilience], [Charmaine Anna Ncube] shares a courageous tale of survival, resilience, and the unyielding spirit of the human soul. The raw honesty and vulnerability woven into the narrative create an intimate connection between author and reader, forging a bond that transcends the boundaries of time and space.Drawing from a deep well of personal growth and healing, [Charmaine Anna Ncube] offers solace and encouragement to those who have faced adversity. Their work serves as a powerful reminder that no matter the hardships endured, there is always light at the end of the tunnel. With unyielding determination, [Charmaine Anna Ncube] demonstrates the transformative power of embracing one's past, finding strength in vulnerability, and charting a course towards a brighter future.In addition to their remarkable literary achievements, [Charmaine Anna Ncube] has become a beacon of inspiration through their advocacy work. They have used their platform to raise awareness about the importance of addressing abuse, trauma, and mental health, fostering a supportive and compassionate community for survivors. Through speaking engagements, workshops, and community outreach, [Your Name] continues to empower individuals to find their voice, reclaim their power, and embark on their own healing journeys.With each stroke of the pen, [Your Name] continues to make an indelible impact on the literary world and the lives of those who encounter their work. Their commitment to authenticity, resilience, and the power of the human spirit is a testament to the extraordinary potential that lies within each and every one of us.[Charmaine Anna Ncube resides in [Poland], where they continue to inspire and uplift through their writing, advocacy, and unwavering dedication to helping others find strength and healing.

CONTENTS

Epigraph

"In the depths of darkness, I discovered my light. Through the pain of silence, I found my voice. And in the power of forgiveness, I unlocked my freedom. This is the story of Charmaine Anna Ncube, a testament to the resilience of the human spirit and the unwavering strength that emerges from the ashes of adversity."

Foreword

In a world where voices often go unheard and the weight of life's challenges can feel insurmountable, it is a privilege to introduce the extraordinary journey of Charmaine Anna Ncube. Her story, captured within the pages of this book, is a testament to the indomitable spirit of the human soul and the transformative power of resilience.As you embark on this poignant narrative, prepare to be immersed in a world that will elicit a myriad of emotions. Charmaine's life is not defined by its hardships alone but by the unwavering determination that carried her through each trial and tribulation. From the depths of abandonment and abuse to the heights of self-discovery and empowerment, her journey unfolds with honesty, vulnerability, and unwavering strength.Through the artistry of her words, Charmaine Anna Ncube invites you into her world, offering a glimpse into the darkest corners of her past and the brightest rays of hope that illuminated her path. It is a journey that illuminates the power of resilience, the significance of finding one's voice, and the transformative nature of forgiveness.As you turn the pages, may you be moved by Charmaine's courage and inspired to embrace your own journey of healing and self-discovery. Her story serves as a reminder that even in the face of seemingly insurmountable challenges, we possess within us the ability to rise, to overcome, and to flourish.I encourage you to approach this narrative with an open heart and mind, prepared to confront the depths of human experience and emerge with a renewed sense of compassion and empathy. Charmaine's story is not just hers alone; it is a mirror reflecting the collective strength and resilience of survivors everywhere.May this book ignite conversations, foster understanding, and spark a transformative change within each reader. Charmaine Anna Ncube's journey is a testament to the unyielding power of the human spirit, reminding us that no matter what we have endured, we have the capacity to rise, to heal, and to rewrite our own stories.With deepest admiration,[CHARMAINE ANNA NCUBE]

Preface

It is with profound vulnerability and immense gratitude that I pen these words as I reflect upon the journey that led me to this very moment. My name is Charmaine Anna Ncube, and the story you are about to embark on is an intimate exploration of my life, one that has been filled with both darkness and light.In sharing my experiences, I aim to shine a spotlight on the often-unspoken struggles that many individuals face behind closed doors. It is my sincere hope that by peeling back the layers of my own journey, others may find solace, strength, and a renewed sense of hope in their own lives.The path I have traversed has been marked by heartache, abandonment, and unspeakable acts of violence. But woven within the fabric of my story are also threads of resilience, healing, and the profound power of the human spirit. Through the darkest of nights, I discovered that within me resided an unwavering light, a light that guided me towards reclaiming my voice and reclaiming my life.This is not a tale solely focused on the pains of the past; rather, it is an exploration of transformation, forgiveness, and the boundless potential that exists within each of us. It is a testament to the strength that arises when we refuse to be defined by our circumstances and instead choose to redefine our own narratives.As you delve into the pages of this book, I invite you to journey alongside me, to witness the rawness of my experiences, and to feel the depth of my emotions. It is my sincerest hope that my story will serve as a catalyst for change, sparking conversations that dismantle the walls of silence and foster a world where survivors are not only heard but believed.It is my deepest intention to foster empathy and understanding, for in understanding one another's journeys, we cultivate a world that is kinder, more compassionate, and more attuned to the needs of those who have endured trauma.I extend my deepest gratitude to each and every reader who embarks on this transformative journey with me. Your willingness to bear witness to my story is a testament to the power of human connection and the potential for growth and healing that exists within us all.With love and resilience,Charmaine Anna Ncube

Acknowledgements

I stand humbled and grateful as I reflect upon the incredible support and love that has surrounded me throughout this transformative journey. To each person who has played a part in shaping my story, I extend my deepest gratitude and appreciation.First and foremost, I want to express my heartfelt thanks to my grandmother, whose unwavering love and care provided me with a safe haven in a tumultuous world. Your strength and resilience have been an inspiration to me, and I am forever grateful for the foundation you laid in my life.To my friends and chosen family, thank you for standing by my side through the darkest of times. Your unwavering support, listening ears, and comforting presence have been a lifeline that helped me navigate the stormy seas of healing. Your belief in me, even when I struggled to believe in myself, has been a beacon of light.I am eternally grateful to the professionals who have guided me on my healing journey. To the therapists, counselors, and advocates who have provided me with a safe space to share my truth and find healing, I extend my deepest appreciation. Your compassion, expertise, and dedication to helping survivors like myself have made an immeasurable impact on my life.To the organizations and support networks that work tirelessly to empower survivors and raise awareness, thank you for your invaluable work. Your commitment to creating a world where voices are heard and healing is possible is an inspiration. I am honored to stand alongside you in this fight.To my editor and publishing team, thank you for believing in the power of my story and for your tireless efforts in bringing it to life. Your guidance, feedback, and expertise have been invaluable, and I am grateful for the opportunity to share my truth with the world.To my readers, I extend my deepest appreciation. Your willingness to listen, learn, and engage with my story is a testament to the power of storytelling and the potential for empathy and understanding. It is my hope that my words resonate with you, offering solace, encouragement, and the courage to face your own journeys with renewed strength.Lastly, I want to express my heartfelt gratitude to my family. Your unwavering love, support, and belief in me have been the foundation upon which I have rebuilt my life. You have stood by me through every triumph and setback, offering a shoulder to lean on and a hand to hold. I am forever grateful for your presence in my life.To all those who have touched my life in countless ways, whether mentioned here or not, please know that your impact has not gone unnoticed. Each act of kindness, every word of encouragement, and every moment of understanding has shaped the person I am today.As I close this chapter of my story, I carry with me the collective strength and resilience of those who have supported me. Together, we stand as a testament to the power of love, compassion, and the unwavering human spirit.With deepest gratitude,Charmaine Anna Ncube

Introduction

"I was born into a world that wasn't kind to me. My parents left me with my grandmother when I was just a baby, and she became my sole caregiver. Life with my grandmother wasn't easy, but I managed to find moments of joy amidst the chaos. However, my childhood took a dark turn when I became the victim of abuse and rape at a young age. The people who were supposed to protect me didn't believe me when I spoke up, and I was left alone to bear the weight of my pain. For years, I suffered in silence, afraid to speak out for fear of being judged or dismissed. The abuse continued, and it shaped the way I saw the world. I felt like I was living in a nightmare, where there was no escape from the constant pain and fear. I turned to self-destructive behaviors to numb the pain, and I pushed away the people who loved me. I felt like I was drowning, and I didn't know how to save myself.But one day, something inside me snapped. I realized that I couldn't keep living my life like this, that I couldn't let my abusers win. I decided to speak out, to share my story with the world. It wasn't easy - in fact, it was one of the hardest things I've ever done. But the response I received was overwhelming. People who had gone through similar experiences reached out to me, offering their support and encouragement. I realized that I wasn't alone, that there were people out there who understood my pain.Slowly but surely, I started to rebuild my life. I found a support system that lifted me up and helped me see that there was more to life than the darkness I had known for so long. I found a therapist who helped me work through my trauma and learn healthy coping mechanisms. I went back to school and discovered a passion for writing. And most importantly, I learned to love myself, scars and all.This is the story of my journey, a journey of survival and resilience. I hope that my story will inspire others to speak out about their own experiences, to know that they are not alone, and to understand that they are deserving of love and happiness. We all have a story to tell, and it's important that we share them - not only for our own healing, but for the healing of others. We are stronger together than we could ever be alone, and I hope that my story can help others find that strength within themselves.Through my struggles, I learned that life can be incredibly difficult, but that it is also incredibly beautiful. There were times when I wanted to give up, but I kept going. I kept pushing forward, even when it felt like I was moving through quicksand. I learned to take each day as it came, to celebrate the small victories and to keep pushing towards my goals. And over time, those small victories added up. As I grew older, I began to see the world in a different light. I saw the beauty in the small things - a sunset, a good cup of coffee, a kind word from a stranger. I started to appreciate the people in my life who had stood by me through the darkest moments, and I made new friends who brought joy and light into my world. I started to see that life could be good, that there was hope for a brighter future.I know that not everyone has the same support system that I was lucky enough to find. But I also know that there is always hope. No matter how dark things may seem, there is always a way forward. It may be a long and difficult road, but there is always a light at the end of the tunnel.This book is not just about me - it's about all of us. It's about the power of the human spirit to endure, to survive, and to thrive. It's about the importance of speaking out and finding our voices, even in the face of overwhelming adversity. And it's about the incredible strength that we all have within us, if only we choose to tap into it.I hope that this book will inspire others to share their own stories, to find their own voices, and to know that they are never alone. Together, we can create a world where survivors are believed, where healing is possible, and where love and kindness reign supreme."

CHAPTER 1 ; THE BEGGINING

I entered this world with little promise. My parents, burdened by the weight of their youth and the shackles of poverty, made the agonizing choice to entrust me to the care of my grandmother. It was in her embrace that I found my sanctuary, a refuge from the storms of life that raged outside her humble abode. Her love became my anchor, grounding me in a world that seemed determined to cast me adrift.Under my grandmother's watchful eye, I flourished. Her presence was a balm to my weary soul, a respite from the chaos that awaited me beyond the threshold of her home. We would weave tales of enchantment and adventure, losing ourselves in the tapestry of imagination. Her stories breathed life into characters and worlds, teaching me lessons that extended far beyond the confines of our humble dwelling.But as the hands of time continued their relentless march, my grandmother's once vibrant spirit began to falter. The signs were subtle at first—a weariness etched upon her face, a fleeting sigh that betrayed the weight she carried upon her frail shoulders. With each passing day, the light within her seemed to dim, leaving behind a void that echoed with the impending loss that loomed over us.It was during this fragile time that my mother resurfaced, emerging from the shadows of her own tumultuous journey. I had yearned for her return, clung to the hope that her presence would mend the fragmented pieces of my identity. But hope, as I soon discovered, can be a cruel mistress.My mother, entangled in the clutches of addiction and tormented by the demons of mental illness, became a tempest that tore through the fragile tapestry of our lives. The reunion I had dreamed of dissolved like mist in the morning sun, replaced by a desolate reality where chaos reigned supreme. I was thrust into a world of unpredictability, where the ground beneath my feet crumbled with each step I took.Abandoned and adrift, I became intimately acquainted with the depths of hunger, both physical and emotional. The pangs of an empty stomach were matched only by the ache in my heart—a hunger for stability, for a love that would hold me steadfast in the face of adversity. Alone, I wandered through the labyrinth of an empty home, the specter of fear my constant companion.In those moments of solitude, when the weight of the world pressed down upon my small shoulders, books became my solace. Within their pages, I discovered an escape, a portal to worlds where heroes rose from the ashes and triumphed over their tribulations. The ink-stained pages became a lifeline, carrying me through the darkest nights and offering glimpses of the light that awaited me beyond the horizon.The trials of my early childhood etched themselves upon my soul, imprinting upon me a resilience that defied the cruel hand fate had dealt. The struggles, the wounds, and the battles fought in the depths of my being molded me into a warrior—a warrior determined to rise above the confines of circumstance, to defy the labels society sought to impose.This chapter marked the genesis of a journey, a journey fraught with adversity, but one that held the promise of transformation and redemption. Little did I know then that the tribulations that awaited me would forge an unbreakable spirit, an indomitable will to reclaim my identity and rewrite the narrative of my life.

CHAPTER 2; BETRAYAL

The dawn of that fateful day bathed the world in a deceptive glow, its rays dancing upon the tapestry of our modest abode. Little did I know that the unfolding hours would etch themselves into the fabric of my existence, leaving scars that time could never fully heal.As my mother's companion entered our home, a veneer of affability veiled the darkness lurking within his soul. His countenance bore an unsettling blend of charm and deceit, his every movement a calculated dance to ensnare the unsuspecting prey. I greeted him with a mixture of curiosity and trepidation, unaware of the storm brewing beneath his charismatic facade.In the absence of my mother, he began to weave his web of malevolence. With each passing moment, his intentions became clearer, his advances growing bolder. It started with a touch, seemingly innocent, but carrying an undercurrent of malice that sent tremors coursing through my vulnerable frame.I stood frozen, a helpless creature ensnared in the snare of a predator. My innocence, once a shield against the world's cruelties, shattered in an instant. The boundaries of my safe haven were breached, and the sanctity of my being violated. In the depths of my young psyche, a cacophony of emotions erupted—fear, confusion, and a profound sense of betrayal.With bated breath, I awaited my mother's return, longing for her protective embrace, hoping she would shield me from the encroaching darkness. But as she reentered the room, her eyes met mine not with compassion, but with disbelief and anger. The words that spilled from her lips pierced my fragile heart like shards of broken glass.Accusations hung heavy in the air, accusing me of weaving a tapestry of lies for mere attention. In that moment, I felt the weight of her disbelief crash upon me, eroding the foundation of trust and love that a child so desperately craves. The depth of her betrayal was a blade that sliced through my soul, leaving me gasping for breath in a world turned upside down.Yet, the horror did not end there. Each passing day ushered in a parade of unfamiliar faces, shadowy figures cloaked in darkness. My mother's companions, driven by their own twisted desires, descended upon our home like vultures drawn to a wounded prey. Their actions spoke louder than any words could, as innocence was shattered anew with each encounter.The nights became an eerie symphony of despair, as the once-familiar sounds of laughter and warmth were replaced by sinister whispers and stifled cries. Within the walls that had witnessed my fleeting moments of joy, I now found myself trapped in a labyrinth of torment, tormented by the hands of those who should have protected me.With each violation, my spirit withered, wilted by the weight of their transgressions. The dictionary of pain expanded within my young mind, its pages filled with words like anguish, sorrow, and anguish. The once-bright colors of my world faded, replaced by a palette of muted greys and endless shades of despair.In my darkest moments, I sought refuge in the solace of night. As the moon cast its gentle glow upon my tear-stained cheeks, I poured my heart into whispered confessions, seeking solace in its silent embrace. The stars above became witnesses to my silent agony, their distant twinkle serving as a reminder that amidst the abyss, a sliver of hope still flickered. The betrayal inflicted upon my tender soul forged a fracture in the tapestry of trust, leaving me adrift in a sea of unanswered questions and unspoken anguish. But even within the depths of my despair, a flame of resilience burned bright—a defiant spark that refused to be extinguished, fueled by the strength born from the crucible of suffering. This chapter marked a turning point, a testament to the indomitable spirit that would guide me through the labyrinth of darkness that lay ahead. It was within the crucible of betrayal that the seeds of survival were sown, preparing me for the arduous journey that awaited—a journey toward healing, redemption, and the reclamation of my stolen innocence.

CHAPTER 3; ALONE

As the shadows lengthened and the echoes of past traumas lingered, I found myself thrust into a desolate world where the ache of loneliness permeated every fiber of my being. The sanctuary of my grandmother's love had slipped through my fingers, leaving me exposed to the harsh winds of abandonment and isolation.In the wake of the storm that raged within our home, my grandmother's health steadily declined, leaving her unable to shield me from the unforgiving reality that awaited. Her once-vibrant spirit dimmed, like a flickering candle fighting against an impending darkness. I watched as her frail body withered, each labored breath a painful reminder of the inevitable.With her weakening grasp on life, the responsibility of caring for me fell into the hands of an absent mother, consumed by her own demons. Her presence became a fleeting illusion, a mere mirage in the barren desert of my existence. Days turned into weeks, and weeks into months, with her sporadic appearances punctuated by empty promises and broken fragments of love.Alone, I navigated the labyrinthine corridors of hunger and fear, a child adrift in a world that seemed indifferent to my plight. The dictionary of loneliness unfolded before me, revealing its cruel definitions in vivid clarity. Isolation, solitude, abandonment—the weight of these words pressed upon my fragile shoulders, threatening to crush my spirit.I sought solace in the recesses of my imagination, where worlds of enchantment and wonder offered respite from the harsh realities that encased me. The worn pages of tattered books became my sanctuary, transporting me to realms where heroes conquered adversity and friendships bloomed like fragile blossoms in a forgotten garden.But even within the refuge of my own mind, the specter of desolation loomed. It whispered in my ear, reminding me that the characters I cherished were figments of fiction, and the warmth they exuded remained beyond my reach. The realization struck me with the force of a thousand blows, deepening the chasm of loneliness that consumed my soul.In the darkest hours of the night, as the world slumbered and dreams took flight, I clung to my pillow, seeking solace in its familiar contours. Tears stained the fabric, each droplet a testament to the silent anguish that coursed through my veins. In the solitude of my tears, I yearned for a comforting touch, a gentle voice to chase away the demons that haunted me.Days turned into nights, and nights into days, the passage of time measured not by clocks or calendars but by the ache within my heart. In the absence of companionship, I befriended the silence, finding solace in its whispered secrets. The dictionary of resilience grew, its pages filled with words like fortitude, determination, and inner strength.Yet, within the depths of my solitude, a flame of hope flickered. It was a fragile ember that refused to be extinguished—a glimmer of light amidst the overwhelming darkness. In the depths of my despair, I discovered a wellspring of strength that resided within me, a resilience that defied the odds.Through the solitary moments, I learned to embrace my own company, to nurture the flickering flame within my soul. I reveled in the beauty of my own thoughts, finding solace in the whispered conversations with my dreams. In the silence, I discovered my own voice, a voice that carried the weight of my experiences and the resilience of my spirit.Alone, but not defeated, I forged a path forward, guided by the flickering flame of resilience that burned within me. In the desolate landscape of loneliness, I learned to seek solace in my own presence, to find strength in the depths of my solitude. And little did I know, the seeds of self-reliance that were sown in those solitary moments would one day blossom into a garden of empowerment, a testament to the unwavering spirit that refused to be broken.

CHAPTER 4; FINDING MY VOICE

In the midst of the suffocating silence that enveloped my existence, a glimmer of hope emerged, beckoning me to explore the depths of my own voice. It was a journey of self-discovery, a quest to unearth the words that had long been suppressed, shackled by fear and the weight of unspoken truths.Within the confines of my solitude, I embarked on an arduous exploration of self-expression. Each word became a brushstroke on the canvas of my soul, painting a vivid portrait of my pain, my resilience, and my unwavering determination to be heard.I turned to the pages of journals, their blank spaces eager to receive the ink that flowed from the depths of my heart. With trembling hands, I poured my emotions onto the paper, releasing the pent-up anguish and reclaiming fragments of my shattered identity. The dictionary of liberation unfolded before me, its words an anthem of defiance against the silence that once suffocated me.Through the ink-stained pages, I found solace, validation, and the first whispers of healing. Each stroke of the pen became a declaration of my existence, a testament to my survival in a world that had tried to extinguish my spirit. The weight of my experiences, once a burden too heavy to bear, transformed into the fuel that ignited the fire of my resilience.But finding my voice extended beyond the private sanctuary of pen and paper. It meant summoning the courage to confront the outside world, to confront those who had turned a blind eye to my pain. With trepidation coursing through my veins, I spoke my truth to those who had doubted, dismissed, and silenced me.Words tumbled from my lips, each syllable a battle cry, challenging the indifference and ignorance that had shrouded my existence. I spoke not only for myself but for the countless others whose voices had been stifled by the darkness of their own stories. The dictionary of advocacy unfolded before me, empowering me to be a catalyst for change, a beacon of hope for those trapped in the shadows.Emotions surged through me as I faced the incredulous faces and hardened hearts that dared to question my truth. Anger ignited within me, fueled by the injustice I had endured, and transformed into a fierce determination to dismantle the walls of silence and ignorance. It was a dance of vulnerability and strength, of raw emotions and unyielding resilience.With each word that escaped my lips, I chipped away at the armor of disbelief, shattering the barriers that had shielded my truth. The dictionary of empowerment became my guiding light, illuminating the path toward self-advocacy and inspiring others to break free from the chains of silence.As I spoke my truth, I realized that my voice held the power to spark empathy, to foster understanding, and to ignite change. It became a beacon of light in the darkest corners of society, illuminating the hidden stories of abuse and resilience that had long been shrouded in silence.But finding my voice was not without its challenges. It required confronting the demons of self-doubt, battling the echoes of victim-blaming and societal stigma. There were moments when my voice wavered, when fear threatened to swallow me whole. Yet, with every setback, I rediscovered my inner strength, my unwavering commitment to rewriting my narrative.Finding my voice was an ongoing journey, an evolution of self-expression and self-empowerment. It was a reminder that my voice mattered, that my experiences were valid, and that I was deserving of love, support, and justice.In the symphony of my words, I found liberation. The dictionary of resilience expanded, its pages adorned with the stories of countless survivors who found solace in their own voices. And as I raised my voice, I became a testament to the indomitable human spirit, a living testament that no matter the depths of darkness, the power of one's voice can prevail. Finding My Voice was a testament to the power of words, the transformational journey of self-expression, and the unwavering spirit that refuses to be silenced. It was a chapter filled with raw emotions, the struggle to overcome self-doubt, and the triumph of reclaiming one's voice in a world that often turns a blind eye. Through the dictionary of liberation and advocacy, the protagonist discovered the strength to confront the shadows of their past and shine a light on the truths that had long been buried. It was a pivotal chapter that marked a turning point in their journey toward healing, resilience, and the pursuit of justice.

CHAPTER 5; MOVING FORWARD

With the echoes of my voice still reverberating in the air, I stood at the precipice of a new chapter in my life. It was a chapter of resilience, growth, and the unwavering commitment to move forward, even in the face of unimaginable adversity.The dictionary of perseverance unfolded before me, its pages filled with words of strength, determination, and the unyielding spirit that refused to be defined by the pain of the past. I took each word to heart, allowing them to infuse my being with a renewed sense of purpose.As I embarked on the path of healing, I knew that it wouldn't be easy. The wounds inflicted upon me ran deep, leaving scars that served as constant reminders of the trauma I had endured. But I was ready to face the challenges head-on, armed with the resilience that had been cultivated within me.Moving forward meant unraveling the tangled threads of my past, untangling the web of pain and reclaiming my identity. It required confronting the emotions that had long been suppressed, allowing myself to feel the full spectrum of joy, sorrow, anger, and hope.In the quiet moments of reflection, I delved into the dictionary of introspection, exploring the depths of my soul and making peace with the fragments of my shattered innocence. It was a delicate dance, navigating the intricate complexities of forgiveness and self-compassion. But with each step, I discovered a newfound strength, a resilience that defied the odds.Moving forward meant surrounding myself with a support system that understood the depths of my journey. I sought solace in the embrace of friends and loved ones who stood by my side, offering a sanctuary of love, empathy, and unwavering support. Their presence became a lifeline, a constant reminder that I was not alone in this battle.The dictionary of connection unfolded before me, its words weaving a tapestry of compassion, understanding, and shared experiences. Together, we found solace in our collective strength, lifting each other up on the darkest of days and celebrating even the smallest victories.But moving forward also meant confronting the legal system, seeking justice for the atrocities that had been inflicted upon me. It was a daunting task, one that required navigating the labyrinthine complexities of the courtroom, the language of the law, and the courage to face my abusers once again.In the dictionary of justice, I found the words to articulate my truth, to demand accountability, and to reclaim my power. The courtroom became a battleground, where I stood as a survivor, an advocate, and a voice for those who had been silenced. It was an emotionally charged journey, as the weight of my testimony collided with the walls of denial and the struggle for justice.But through it all, I remained steadfast. The dictionary of determination became my guiding light, fuelling my resolve to fight for what was right, to ensure that my story, and the stories of countless others, would not be forgotten or dismissed.Moving forward was not a linear path. It was filled with setbacks, moments of doubt, and the occasional stumble. But with each setback, I rediscovered my resilience, my unwavering commitment to rewrite my narrative, and my refusal to be defined by the traumas of the past.As this chapter came to a close, I realized that moving forward wasn't just about leaving the past behind. It was about integrating my experiences into the fabric of my being, using them as stepping stones to a brighter future. The dictionary of transformation unfolded before me, its words a testament to the strength and beauty that can emerge from the depths of darkness. Moving Forward marked a pivotal moment in my journey. It was a chapter of resilience, healing, and the unyielding determination to build a life that was defined by love, compassion, and the unwavering belief in the power of the human spirit. As I turned the page, I did so with hope, knowing that the dictionary of possibilities lay before me, ready to be explored one word at a time.

CHAPTER 6; THE POWER OF FORGIVENESS

In the depths of my healing journey, I encountered a concept that tested the very essence of my being: forgiveness. It was a chapter steeped in introspection, vulnerability, and the profound realization that forgiveness was not a sign of weakness, but an act of immense strength.The dictionary of forgiveness unfolded before me, its pages adorned with words of mercy, compassion, and the liberation that comes from releasing the shackles of resentment. It was a daunting task, to face the demons of my past and embrace the transformative power of forgiveness. But I knew that it was an essential step towards my own inner peace and growth.Forgiveness was not an easy path to tread. It required confronting the wounds that had been inflicted upon me, acknowledging the pain and injustice that had shaped my life. It demanded that I delve into the dictionary of empathy, seeking to understand the complexities of human nature and the circumstances that had led others astray.As I navigated the intricate landscapes of forgiveness, I found solace in the dictionary of compassion. It became my guide, teaching me to extend kindness not only to others, but to myself as well. I learned that forgiveness was not about condoning or forgetting the past, but about releasing the heavy burden of resentment that weighed upon my soul.In the dictionary of introspection, I explored the depths of my own heart, seeking to uncover the wounds and insecurities that had clouded my capacity to forgive. It was a journey of self-reflection, as I confronted the layers of anger, fear, and betrayal that had built up over time. Through tears and moments of raw vulnerability, I unraveled the intricate tapestry of my emotions, embracing the complexity of forgiveness.The power of forgiveness lay not only in its ability to heal the wounds of the past, but also in its capacity to redefine relationships. In the dictionary of reconciliation, I discovered the transformative potential of forgiveness. It offered the opportunity to mend broken bonds, to bridge the gaps that had been widened by pain and mistrust. It required courage and vulnerability to engage in open dialogue, to express my truth, and to listen with empathy to the perspectives of others.But forgiveness was not a one-time act. It was a continuous practice, a commitment to release resentment and cultivate compassion in every aspect of my life. It required resilience, as I faced triggers and moments of relapse. It demanded self-compassion, as I navigated the complexities of my own healing journey.In the dictionary of liberation, I found the freedom that comes from forgiving others and myself. It was a profound realization that holding onto anger and resentment only perpetuated the cycle of pain. By embracing forgiveness, I broke free from the chains of the past, opening myself up to new possibilities, and paving the way for personal growth and transformation.The power of forgiveness was not without its challenges. It required strength, perseverance, and a deep well of compassion. But through the dictionary of resilience, I discovered that forgiveness was an act of radical self-love. It allowed me to reclaim my power, to transcend the victimhood that had defined me for far too long, and to step into a future where healing, growth, and joy were within my reach. The Power of Forgiveness marked a significant milestone in my journey of self-discovery. It was a chapter of surrender, acceptance, and the profound understanding that forgiveness was not a gift bestowed upon others, but a gift I gave to myself. As I closed the chapter, I carried with me the newfound freedom that comes from embracing forgiveness, ready to embrace the future with an open heart and renewed sense of purpose.

CHAPTER 7; SPEAKING OUT

The pen trembled in my hand as I prepared to write the next chapter of my life. It was a chapter that required unwavering courage, resilience, and the unwavering determination to break the suffocating silence that had enveloped me for far too long. It was time to speak out.In the dictionary of bravery, I sought inspiration and strength. I knew that sharing my story would not be an easy task. It meant exposing my deepest vulnerabilities, reliving painful memories, and risking judgment and disbelief. But I also knew that my voice held the power to inspire, to educate, and to create change. It was a power I could no longer keep locked away.As I embarked on the journey of speaking out, I discovered the dictionary of empowerment. It became my guiding light, reminding me that my voice mattered, that my experiences were valid, and that I had the right to be heard. I embraced the emotions that swirled within me – fear, anger, and a profound sense of injustice – and transformed them into a driving force for advocacy and healing.With each word I spoke, with each sentence I penned, I shattered the chains of silence that had bound me for so long. It was a cathartic release, an act of reclaiming my agency and asserting my truth. The dictionary of liberation expanded before me, its pages filled with words of empowerment, resilience, and the audacity to challenge the status quo.As I shared my story, I encountered the dictionary of validation. It was within the empathetic ears of those who listened that I found solace and affirmation. They offered validation to the pain I had endured, and their support became a balm for my wounded soul. Their belief in my truth bolstered my resolve to continue speaking out, no matter the obstacles.The dictionary of advocacy became my compass, guiding me towards platforms where my voice could be amplified. I joined support groups, engaged in community dialogues, and became an advocate for survivors of abuse and injustice. In the dictionary of empathy, I discovered the power of collective voices united in the pursuit of justice and healing.Speaking out was not without its challenges. The dictionary of resilience taught me to weather the storm of backlash, skepticism, and victim-blaming. It required me to cultivate inner strength, to hold firm in my conviction, and to persevere in the face of adversity. But the dictionary of resilience also reminded me that my voice was a beacon of hope for others who may be trapped in silence, urging me to press forward.Through the dictionary of catharsis, I found release and healing. Speaking out allowed me to shed the weight of secrecy, to unearth buried emotions, and to embark on a journey of self-discovery and self-acceptance. It was a transformative process, as I discovered the power of my own vulnerability and the ability to turn pain into purpose.In the dictionary of impact, I witnessed the ripple effects of my words. Survivors reached out, sharing their own stories of resilience and healing. Strangers became allies in the fight against abuse and injustice. Institutions and communities began to listen, to reflect, and to enact change. My voice became a catalyst for societal transformation.Speaking Out was a testament to the indomitable spirit of survivors. It was a chapter that redefined silence as a breeding ground for injustice and gave rise to a symphony of voices demanding change. As I closed the chapter, I carried within me the knowledge that my voice had the power to create a world where survivors were believed, supported, and empowered.

CHAPTER 8; THE POWER OF THE COMMUNITY

In the vast tapestry of my healing journey, there was a pivotal chapter that illuminated the profound impact of community. It was within the embrace of a supportive network that I discovered the dictionary of belonging, and the transformative power it held.The pages of this chapter were adorned with the dictionary of empathy, as I found myself surrounded by individuals who had walked similar paths of pain and resilience. They understood the depths of my wounds, the complexities of my emotions, and the strength required to rebuild shattered lives. Together, we formed a collective tapestry of survivors, united in our pursuit of healing.Within the dictionary of compassion, I encountered kindred souls who extended their hearts and hands to lift me from the depths of despair. They listened without judgment, providing a safe space where vulnerability flourished. Their compassion became a soothing balm for my wounded spirit, reminding me that I was not alone on this journey.The dictionary of support offered me a refuge, a place where I could lean on others when my own strength faltered. It was through support groups, therapy sessions, and online communities that I discovered the power of shared experiences. Together, we wove a tapestry of resilience, interlacing our stories and empowering one another to navigate the complexities of healing.Within the dictionary of camaraderie, I witnessed the strength of unity. Survivor-led organizations and advocacy groups provided a platform for collective action, amplifying our voices and demanding systemic change. Through grassroots movements and awareness campaigns, we fought for justice, education, and prevention, weaving threads of resilience into the fabric of society.In the dictionary of empowerment, I found courage to speak my truth boldly and unapologetically. The unwavering support of my community bolstered my confidence, giving rise to a newfound sense of agency. Together, we challenged the narrative of victimhood, reclaiming our stories and rewriting the script of our lives.The dictionary of resilience unfolded before me, teaching me that healing was not a linear journey but a testament to the human spirit's capacity to rise above adversity. As we shared our triumphs and setbacks, we celebrated each milestone reached and offered solace in times of setback. Our collective resilience became a beacon of hope, illuminating the path forward.Within the dictionary of advocacy, I discovered the strength to create change beyond my personal healing. I joined forces with my community to raise awareness, educate others, and challenge societal norms that perpetuated abuse and injustice. Together, we sparked conversations, held institutions accountable, and nurtured a culture of empathy and understanding.The power of community transformed my healing journey into a tapestry of interconnected lives, woven together by threads of compassion, support, and shared experiences. Each person I encountered became a brushstroke on the canvas of my story, coloring it with the hues of resilience, solidarity, and hope.The Power of Community encapsulated the realization that healing was not a solitary pursuit but a collective endeavor. It celebrated the beauty of human connection and the profound impact that community support could have on individual and societal healing. As I closed this chapter, I carried with me a deep gratitude for the interconnectedness that had shaped my journey, and a renewed commitment to fostering communities of compassion and resilience.

CHAPTER 9; THE JOURNEY CONTINUES

The Journey ContinuesAs I turned the page to Chapter 9, I found myself standing at the precipice of a new beginning. The ink of my story glistened with anticipation, for this chapter was not an end, but a continuation of the tapestry I had woven so far.Within the dictionary of perseverance, I discovered an unwavering determination to keep moving forward. The path of healing had been strewn with obstacles and moments of doubt, but I refused to let them define me. With each step, I embraced the challenges as opportunities for growth, fortifying my spirit with resilience.The dictionary of self-discovery unfolded before me, beckoning me to delve deeper into the recesses of my being. I embarked on a journey of introspection, unearthing layers of buried emotions and untapped potential. It was within the depths of self-exploration that I found the courage to confront my past, to peel away the scars and discover the essence of my true self.In the dictionary of healing modalities, I sought out various avenues to nurture my mind, body, and soul. From therapy sessions and support groups to meditation, yoga, and creative outlets, I embraced a holistic approach to my well-being. Each modality became a brushstroke on the canvas of my healing, adding depth and color to my journey.The dictionary of forgiveness beckoned me to release the burdens of resentment and anger that had weighed heavily on my heart. It was not an easy path, for forgiveness required immense strength and vulnerability. But as I traversed the terrain of forgiveness, I discovered that it was not about condoning the actions of those who had hurt me, but freeing myself from the shackles of bitterness and reclaiming my power.Within the dictionary of self-care, I learned the art of nourishing my body, mind, and soul. I embraced acts of self-love, honoring my needs and setting healthy boundaries. From indulging in simple pleasures to engaging in practices that replenished my spirit, I recognized the importance of tending to my well-being with unwavering devotion.The dictionary of connection opened its pages to reveal the beauty of building meaningful relationships. I sought out authentic connections with kindred spirits who understood the intricacies of my journey. Together, we forged bonds of trust, vulnerability, and unconditional support, creating a tapestry of friendship and love that nurtured my soul.Within the dictionary of purpose, I discovered a calling to advocate for change and inspire others on their own healing journeys. I shared my story with unwavering honesty, shedding light on the dark corners of abuse and trauma. Through writing, speaking engagements, and community outreach, I aimed to empower survivors, dismantle stigmas, and foster a culture of compassion and understanding.As the pages of this chapter unfolded, I embraced the uncertainty of the path ahead. The journey continued, and with each passing moment, I realized that healing was not a destination, but an ongoing process of growth and self-discovery. I approached the future with a renewed sense of hope, knowing that within me resided the strength, resilience, and unwavering determination to face whatever challenges lay ahead.In the tapestry of my life, Chapter 9 was a testament to the power of perseverance, self-discovery, forgiveness, self-care, connection, and purpose. It embodied the beauty of embracing the journey, with all its triumphs and tribulations, and finding meaning in every step taken.As I turned the final page of this chapter, I felt a profound sense of gratitude for the lessons learned, the strength gained, and the souls intertwined with mine. With the flicker of anticipation in my heart, I eagerly awaited the unfolding of the next chapter, knowing that the journey would continue to shape and mold me into the resilient, empowered, and whole person I was destined to become.